No Reservation Required

a book by

PATRICK FISHER

photography & layout by

EDYTA KUCIAPA

Table of Contents

No Reservation Required

Hello Friends!

First off, I would like to start out with thanking each and every one of you for purchasing a copy of this book. I know times are tough for everyone but the fact that you spent a little extra on me means a lot. So don't worry, you are in for a real big treat.

There are a lot of recipes in this book that will complement everyone's taste buds. Whether you are looking to cook your other half a nice dinner or you're just trying to feed the kids, I've got a recipe for you! If you're planning a dinner party, I have you covered with a three-course dinner! Fellas, I can't guarantee you'll get the ladies after dinner but you will surely give them a good meal. You often hear the saying that food is a way to a man's heart, well the same maybe true for the gals! Parents, you may actually get the kids to eat your cooking, which is always a good thing. There are different options for all of these occasions, so I invite you to flip through this book and find recipes that will work for your time, effort and budget.

A bit of advice for all you aspiring people who want to work in the culinary field, just remember that you don't need a degree or a piece of paper to tell you that you can cook, you just have to work at it. Watch a cooking show or two and get your butt in the kitchen and try to mix stuff together and make it work. Challenge yourself by creating a dish you have never even heard of, follow a recipe and improvise as you go along. All you need is a key ingredient, then you just build around it. If it tastes good, write it down and maybe you can make a book like this at some point in your life. But then again, you could just keep eating my food in this book... yeah, just stick to that plan, I like that plan better.

Well alright, we should get cooking now, shouldn't we? Yes, I have discovered I talk too much, but what can I say...it runs in the family.

You see, **No Reservation Required** isn't just about food, recipes are intertwined with my personal stories and different experiences I had while making these dishes. Plus there's some food that's just plain yummy that you need to try. So let's work together, step by step, chapter by chapter and get the food on the table. The recipes in this book are sure to become a family favorite and there's even a chapter for all of you coffee lovers. I am a big coffee drinker myself but coffee houses have gotten so expensive that it's time to make some of your favorites at homc. I have also put together a kid friendly section in this book.

If you read my first book, thank you! This second time around, I've had more time to reflect and put everything together one step at a time and let me tell you I am honored to be the author of such a wonderful piece of culinary delight for you. This is bound to get you off your feet and in the kitchen.

The most important thing to remember, is that you don't need a reservation to have a delicious, restaurant-worthy meal at home!

So in the words of Peter Pan, here we go off to never never land— I mean **food land**—I mean the kitchen! See you in chapter one!

Sincerely,

Pat

Dear Friends,

I would like to start by saying good morning! So are you ready to whip up some yummy food to start your day off right? I thought you would, be so there are quite a few choices to choose from. I've got a great spin-off on a classic; the **Salted Caramel French Toast**, or rustic dish; the **Old-fashioned Italian Omelette** and some originals like **My Big Fat Italian Uncle's Breakfast Sandwich** and of course the **Elvis Smoothie** which you are sure to love.

Now how about you pour yourself a cup of coffee and let's get this morning started. READY -- BREAK -- FAST!

Sincerely,

Pat

Morning Specials

MY BIG FAT ITALIAN UNCLE'S BREAKFAST SANDWICH 10

JERSEY SHORE PANINI 12

SALTED CARAMEL FRENCH TOAST 14

OLD-FASHIONED ITALIAN OMELETTE 16

ELVIS SMOOTHIE 18

CHOCOLATE BANANA SMOOTHIE 20

My Big Fat Italian Uncle's Breakfast Sandwich

THE INGREDIENTS

2 English muffins,
one for each sandwich

2 slices of thick slices
of pancetta, one for
each sandwich

2 slices of Provolone cheese,
one for each sandwich

2 eggs

THE STEPS

1. Slice your English muffins in half
    and toast in a toaster oven to brown.

2. In a small frying pan, cook the eggs
    over easy one at a time and cover.

3. When the muffin is finished toasting,
    start to layer the base sandwich with
    the cheese, pancetta, and egg and
    top it off with the top half of the
    English muffin.

SERVES 2

ARE YOU SICK AND TIRED OF THAT BORING OLD EGG McMUFFIN FROM
THAT FAST FOOD PLACE DOWN THE STREET? *YES!*
WOULD YOU CARE TO TRY SOMETHING DIFFERENT? *YES!*
OKAY, WELL BOY HAVE I GOT A TREAT FOR YOU! (DRUM ROLL PLEASE...)
I GIVE YOU STRAIGHT OFF THE PRESS MY BIG FAT ITALIAN UNCLE'S BREAKFAST SANDWICH!

Jersey Shore Panini

THE INGREDIENTS

2 ciabatta rolls cut in half

2 slices of Cheddar cheese

2 slices of pork roll (for the Jersey natives) or Italian sausage patties

2 eggs

THE STEPS

1. Cook the pork roll or sausage according to the directions on the packaging and set aside.

2. Next, cook up those eggs over easy but let the yolk cook a little while longer.

3. Place one of the ciabatta rolls on a medium skillet and let it "tan."

4. Top with the pork roll or sausage, cheese and press the sandwich using another pan to make it flat like a panini should be and serve with the egg.

5. Repeat for second sandwich.

6. Serve and eat!

SERVES 2

WHO DOESN'T LOVE A GOOD OLD FASHION PANINI? I PERSONALLY
COULD EAT ONE AT EVERY MEAL SO HERE IS A GREAT BREAKFAST ONE.
IF YOU DON'T HAVE A PANINI MAKER IT'S ALL GOOD!!! JUST IMPROVISE
WITH TWO FRYING PANS; ONE FOR COOKING AND ONE FOR WHACKING.
JUST REMEMBER, FOR BEST RESULTS USE CIABATTA ROLLS.

FRENCH TOAST DOESN'T COME AROUND OFTEN IN MY HOUSEHOLD. WE TEND TO SKIP OUT ON A LEGIT BREAKFAST BUT IF WE DO EAT IT WE TEND TO LEAN TOWARD THIS BABY RIGHT HERE! SO GRAB A CUP OF COFFEE AND LET'S GET OUT THAT OLD GRIDDLE YOU HAVEN'T USED IN YEARS AND LET'S IMPRESS SOMEONE :)

Salted Caramel French Toast

THE STEPS

1. Beat eggs, milk, and cinnamon together. Whisk until well blended.

2. Dip each slice of bread into the egg mixture.

3. Melt butter over a large skillet on medium-high heat and heat 4 slices at a time in the pan.

4. Fry until brown on both sides, flipping the bread when necessary.

5. Now for the sauce, melt butter or margarine in a medium skillet over medium heat.

6. Stir in brown sugar and cinnamon. Bring to a slow boil and simmer about 5 minutes, stirring frequently.

7. Serve the sauce over the top of the french toast and serve immediately.

SERVES 4

THE INGREDIENTS

FRENCH TOAST

4 eggs

$^2/_3$ cup milk

2 teaspoons of cinnamon

2 tbsp butter

8 thick slices of 2-day-old bread, better if slightly stale

SAUCE

½ stick of butter

1 cup brown sugar

½ tsp cinnamon

Old-Fashioned Italian Omelette

THE INGREDIENTS

1 spin of olive oil

1 tsp minced garlic

Dash of salt and pepper

3 eggs

1 slice of prosciutto, diced

1 slice of capricola ham, diced

1 basil leaf, diced

1 slice of Provolone cheese

THE STEPS

1. In a small bowl, crack the eggs and scramble with a fork, add in the salami, ham, basil and set aside.

2. In a medium frying pan, add the olive oil, garlic, salt and pepper and cook on medium-high heat until the garlic is lightly browned.

3. Add in the egg mixture and cook for about 25 seconds and flip.

4. Cook another 20 seconds.

5. Place the slice of cheese on the egg and fold the egg over.

6. Plate and eat.

MAKES 1 OMELETTE

I AM SURE YOU HAVE ALL HEARD OF AN ELVIS SANDWICH AT SOME POINT IN YOUR LIFE. WELL, I HAVE MIXED IT INTO A DRINK! DON'T DITCH IT UNTIL YOU HAVE TRIED IT, I PROMISE YOU WILL NOT BE DISAPPOINTED! OH AND MAKE SURE NOT TO PUT THE BREAD IN THE SMOOTHIE, IT WON'T TASTE VERY GOOD.. YEAH I TRIED THAT.

Elvis
Smoothie

THE STEPS

1. Place all of the ingredients: the banana, ice cubes, bacon, peanut butter, chocolate syrup and half and half in a blender.

2. Blend until smooth.

3. Divide into 2-3 glasses.

4. Serve immediately.

SERVES 2-3

THE INGREDIENTS

1 banana, peeled

8 ice cubes

2 slices of cooked crispy bacon

3 tbsp of peanut butter

1 tbsp of chocolate syrup

¼ cup Half and Half

Chocolate Banana Smoothie

THE STEPS

1. In a blender, add the ice, banana, vanilla extract, hot chocolate mix, and the lite cream and blend on the smoothie option. (If your blender doesn't have a smoothie option, the closest is frappe).

2. Pour into two glasses.

3. Top with the whipped cream.

4. Using a grater, grate the chocolate bar over top of the whipped cream, or drizzle chocolate syrup like in the photo to the left.

5. Ready to serve!

SERVES 2

THE INGREDIENTS

SMOOTHIE

8 ice cubes

1 banana

Dash of vanilla extract

1 (.25 oz) packet of hot chocolate mix

½ cup of Half and Half

TOPPING

Whipped cream

Bite-size chocolate bar (for shaving)

Chocolate syrup

CHAPTER TWO

Dear Friends,

Well its noon, you know what that means. LUNCHTIME.

I know, I know, you feel like we just made breakfast. Yeah, it sucks cooking all these meals by yourself, but remember, I got your back! Which means we should cook something yummy... So I was thinking we cook you and your family some **Cheddar and Broccoli Soup** with a **Panini**... sounds good right?

If I had to choose a favorite meal of the week it would most likely be lunch on a weekend. Everything is so relaxed when you're off from work, especially when it's a cold winter, the best thing to make is soup! It makes the whole house just smell wonderful! During Christmas time we usually make soup or stew on a Saturday and it just makes you feel so warm inside, we watch Christmas movies on TV and I am usually in the kitchen every ten minutes stirring up the soup or stew. We cry, we laugh, there really is nowhere else I would rather be on a weekend and I love every minute of it! I just love everything about the time of year — well, minus the shopping...so anyway this one is for you!

Lets Cook!

Pat

Lunch Specials

HOUSE SALAD 26

CHEDDAR &
BROCCOLI SOUP 28

CREAM OF
CHICKEN SOUP 30

PROSCIUTTO &
PROVOLONE PANINI 32

ITALIAN LOVER'S PANINI 34

BEEF STEW WITH
WINE & FRESH HERBS 36

FRENCH BREAD PIZZA
FOR A CROWD 38

House
Salad

SALAD

1 romaine heart

1 cooked chicken
tender breast

¼ cup Mozzarella cheese

4 banana pepper rings,
chopped

1 slice of white bread,
toasted

HOUSE DRESSING

Olive oil

Lemon juice

Parmesan cheese

THE STEPS

1. On a medium cutting board, chop
   the lettuce and place in a large bowl.

2. Top with the banana peppers and
   croutons.

3. Add in the cheese and mix together
   using a large spoon.

4. In a small bowl, mix the salad
   dressing ingredients.

5. Combine the dressing with the
   salad and toss.

6. Serve in salad bowls and enjoy!

SERVES 1

ONE OF THE SIMPLEST THINGS TO MAKE, A SALAD CAN BE WHIPPED UP WITHIN MINUTES AND IT LENDS ITSELF FOR COUNTLESS COMBINATIONS. TAKE MY SUGGESTIONS BUT FEEL FREE TO EXPERIMENT ON YOUR OWN! :)

THIS BEEF STEW IS SURE TO GET YOUR TASTE BUDS PUMPING! IT HAS COME TO BE ONE OF MY CLASSIC DISHES FOR A COLD WINTERS' NIGHT... JUST REMEMBER IT TAKES A FEW HOURS TO MAKE SO MAKE SURE TO MAKE IT DURING THE WEEKEND.

Beef Stew with Wine and Fresh Herbs

THE STEPS

1. In a large STOCKPOT, on medium heat, combine the butter and olive oil. Add in the thyme and bay leaves.

2. Pour the flour into a mixing bowl, add in the beef using your hands and make sure the beef is covered in the flour.

3. Transfer the beef into the saucepan and cook until the beef is browned on both sides.

4. Add in the wine. ALL OF IT.

5. Using a wooden spoon, gather the excess flour off the bottom of the pot and put heat on medium-low. (If the stew is not thick enough, fill an 8 oz glass with cold water and add a tablespoon of cornstarch. Mix well and pour into pot).

6. Slice and cube the potatoes.

7. Add all of the veggies into the pot and let cook on medium-low for about two hours. Stir occasionally.

8. Serve and eat!

SERVES 8-10
PREP 10 MINUTES
COOK 2 HOURS
TOTAL 2 HOURS 10 MINUTES

THE INGREDIENTS

1 stick of margarine

2 tbsp of olive oil

4 sprigs of thyme

2 bay leaves

2 lbs of cubed beef, seasoned with salt and pepper

1 cup flour

1 bottle of red wine

2 (32 oz) beef stock

2 sticks of celery, sliced ½ inch thick

2 large carrots, sliced 1 inch

4 yukon gold potatoes

Cheddar and Broccoli Soup

THE INGREDIENTS

1 large whole broccoli floret

1 can of sliced potatoes

2 cups of fresh Cheddar cheese, shredded

1 (32 oz) chicken stock

Salt and pepper to taste

1 large bay leaf

1 tbsp minced garlic

1 stick of butter

THE STEPS

1. In a large food processor, add the potatoes, broccoli, and ONE cup of the chicken stock. Process for 15 seconds. Set aside.

2. Meanwhile, in a 3-quart pot, melt the butter over medium-high heat and add in the salt and pepper, bay leaf, and garlic. Cook until garlic is browned.

3. Add in the chicken stock and the broccoli mixture. Cook for about 15 minutes and serve in bowls. Top with the shredded Cheddar cheese.

SERVES 6-8
PREP 10 MINUTES
ACTIVE 15 MINUTES
TOTAL 25 MINUTES

THIS RECIPE IS A NEW EDITION TO THE MANY SOUPS I MAKE IN THE WINTERTIME FOR MY LOVED ONES. IT HAS BECOME ONE OF MY GREATEST, MOST HEALTHIEST THINGS I MAKE AND IT IS SO EASY TO DO! IT IS GUARANTEED TO IMPRESS ALL OF YOUR GUESTS.

FOR A MEXICAN TWIST, SUBSTITUTE TACO BLEND CHEESE FOR THE CHEDDAR CHEESE.

Cream of Chicken Soup

THE INGREDIENTS

1 tbsp margarine

1 tbsp minced garlic

Large handful of fresh thyme

3 cups of chicken stock

1 cup of Half and Half

Salt and pepper to taste

2 cups of cooked, chopped and diced chicken breast

THE STEPS

1. In a 3-quart pot, melt the butter over medium-high heat. Add in the garlic and thyme and cook until the garlic is browned.

2. Stir in the chicken stock and heat for 5 minutes.

3. Add in the Half and Half stirring constantly.

4. Season with salt and pepper and add in the cooked chicken. Heat for additional 5 minutes but lower the heat to medium-low.

5. Serve and enjoy!

SERVES 6-8
PREP 8 MINUTES
ACTIVE 22 MINUTES
TOTAL 30 MINUTES

AS A KID I WAS ALWAYS FOND OF THE CONDENSED SOUPS IN THE CAN BUT AS I HAVE GROWN, MY TASTE BUDS HAVE CHANGED AND I AM NO LONGER AFFILIATED WITH THOSE! I ENJOY MAKING MY OWN SOUPS, IT GIVES ME A FEEL OF ACCOMPLISHMENT AFTER MAKING IT — LIKE I MADE THAT? WHAT NOW? (INSIDE JOKE). TO SAY THE LEAST, THIS SOUP WILL NO LONGER MAKE YOU WANT TO GET THE CANNED STUFF.

THIS IS A GREAT LUNCH FOR A FAMILY OF FOUR. I RECOMMEND SERVING IT WITH ONE OF THE SOUPS IN THIS CHAPTER AS WELL FOR A WEEKEND LUNCH AND THE KIDS WILL LOVE IT! HOWEVER, IT'S A 'LIL SPICY SO IF YOU'RE NOT A FAN OF SPICY STUFF, YOU CAN JUST SUBSTITUTE THE CAPRICOLA FOR PROSCIUTTO. AND HEY, IF YOU DON'T HAVE A PANINI PRESS YOU CAN USE A FRYING PAN AND A SMALLER PAN, COOKING THE PANINI ON THE LARGER PAN AND PRESSING DOWN WITH THE BACK OF THE SMALLER ONE.

Prosciutto & Provolone Panini with Tomato Herb Spread

THE STEPS

1. In a small bowl, add all of the tomato spread ingredients and mix well.

2. Spread the tomato mixture using a spatula evenly across four of the slices of ciabatta bread.

3. Place the meat and cheese on the other four slices of bread.

4. Assemble the sandwich together and place it on the panini press.

5. Cook until browned on top and bottom.

6. Serve with soup for a hearty lunch!

SERVES 4

THE INGREDIENTS

SANDWICH

8 slices of ciabatta bread

8 slices of prosciutto

4 slices of Mozzarella cheese

TOMATO HERB SPREAD

4 tbsp tomato paste

Dash of minced garlic

Dash of rosemary, fresh or dried

Dash of thyme, fresh or dried

Handful of Pecorino Romano cheese

Dash of olive oil

Italian Lover's Panini

THE INGREDIENTS

2 ciabatta rolls, sliced lengthwise

2 tbsp olive oil

1 tbsp red wine vinegar

2 slices of Provolone cheese, cut in half

4 slices of Genoa salami, sliced thin

4 slices of capricola, sliced thin

2 slices of prosciutto

4 banana pepper rings

2 tbsp butter for cooking

THE STEPS

1. Slice the roll lengthwise and set aside for a moment.

2. In a small bowl, mix together the olive oil and vinegar.

3. Using a pastry brush, brush the inside of each roll.

4. Layer each sandwich with a slice of provolone, 2 slices of Genoa salami, 2 slices of capricola, and one slice of prosciutto.

5. Heat the skillet with butter on medium-low, add the 2 sandwiches then press using a pan. Cook 3 minutes per side.

6. Serve with a soup or chips.

MAKES 2 SANDWICHES

THIS IS EVERY ITALIAN'S DREAM LUNCH!
IT'S PACKED WITH ALL THE BEST ITALIAN
MEATS AND OF COURSE WHAT'S AN ITALIAN
TO DO WITHOUT HIS OR HER PROVOLONE
CHEESE ON THIS BEAUTIFUL CREATION OF
A SANDWICH?

French Bread Pizza for a Crowd

THE STEPS

1. Turn on the broiler.

2. In a medium bowl, mix the olive oil, basil, tomato paste and garlic and let it all soak together. Set aside.

3. Slice the bread in half lengthwise and top with the tomato herb mixture.

4. Top with the Mozzarella cheese.

5. Broil until browned, for about 1 minute. (Keep an eye on it, every broiler is different and you don't want it to burn).

6. Wait for a minute or two before you are going to serve it and cut into slices.

7. Hope you love it, I know you will!

SERVES 4

THE INGREDIENTS

1 large ciabatta loaf

3 tbsp of olive oil

3 basil leaves, chopped

1 can of Italian herb tomato paste

1 tsp minced garlic

5 slices of fresh Mozzarella cheese

ocktail
Lounge

Dear Friends,

DON'T DRINK AND DRIVE

I am not a big drinker, but I do enjoy entertaining
and it always goes hand in hand with the territory,
so I always have to be prepared.

We are currently looking at putting in a four-person
bar into our house so I thought I would put some
cocktails into this book to please everyone's needs!
If you're not a drinker, don't worry you can still enjoy all
of the drinks in this section, just take out the alcohol.

So what do you say we relax and mingle with those
guests? Remember don't drink alone or you are
considered an AAA Member and I'm not talking
the Travel One! Ha-ha!

Cheers!

Pat

Happy Hour Drink Specials

Shirley Lost
Her Temple

THE INGREDIENTS

¼ cup ginger ale

1 splash of cranberry juice

1 shot of cherry vodka

2 ice cubes

THE STEPS

1. In a cocktail shaker, combine all ingredients and shake. (Make sure to put the lid on).

2. Pour into a wine glass.

SERVES 1

THIS DRINK IS SIMILAR TO THE CLASSIC SHIRLEY TEMPLE BUT I HAVE MADE IT MY OWN BY ADDING IN A LITTLE VODKA TO THE TRADITIONAL MIX.

THIS DRINK IS HOW YOU FEEL WALKING DOWN THE STREET AND SEEING THIS BEAUTIFUL WOMAN WALKING TOWARDS YOU. GUYS YOU KNOW WHAT I'M TALKING ABOUT! YOU GOT THAT SONG IN YOUR HEAD, YOU START SWEATING AND SHE IS STILL A FEW FEET AWAY FROM YOU. THEN YOU JUST LOOK HER IN THE EYES AND FOR ONE SECOND YOUR EYES MEET IN THE NIGHT... YOU GET THOSE MILLISECOND GOOSE BUMPS AND BAM! YOU GET A MIDNIGHT FEVER...

A Midnight
Fever

THE STEPS

1. Wet the top of a martini glass.

2. Sugar the rim.

3. Add in the sparkling apple juice and orange juice.

4. Followed by the vodka.

5. Serve and Enjoy!

SERVES 1

THE INGREDIENTS

¼ cup of sparkling apple juice

$1/3$ cup of orange juice

1 tbsp vodka

Sugar for the rim

Waking Up in Vegas

THE INGREDIENTS

4 ice cubes

½ cup of orange juice

¼ cup of cranberry juice

1 shot of vodka

Orange peel for topping

THE STEPS

1. In a cocktail shaker, combine the ice cubes, orange juice, cranberry juice and vodka. Mix well.

2. In a tall glass, add in the ice and fill up with the drink.

3. Garnish with orange peel.

SERVES 1

NOW THIS ONE IS FOR ALL THOSE PEOPLE THAT DRINK A LITTLE TOO MUCH AND CAN'T REMEMBER WHAT HAPPENED THE NIGHT BEFORE. WELL, AFTER GETTING DRUNK SO MUCH YOU'RE GOING TO END UP DOING SOMETHING SILLY, LIKE IN THE HANGOVER MOVIE, SO LET'S NOT LET THIS HAPPEN!

CHAPTER FOUR

KIDS IN THE KITCHEN

Dear Parents,

If your younger ones haven't eaten or liked anything yet, they will be pretty happy eating and helping mommy and daddy in the kitchen. These are all kid friendly recipes which stem from junk food favorites, except they're not! I've cut down on a lot of bad stuff to make these recipes more kid friendly and healthy. For example, the cheese fries are not your typical cheese fries; they are made with a healthy but more expensive cheese called Pecorino Romano. It's actually made from sheep's milk so it has a lot less fat then any of the average cheeses.

So kids, come on over and let's cook some food with mommy and daddy and help them save money so you can get a bigger Christmas present!!

Ready, set, COOK!

Pat

Kid's Menu

SO DARN GOOD CHICKEN NUGGETS 54

ROSEMARY BALSAMIC INFUSED QUESADILLA 56

CHICKEN LO MEIN 58

PARMESAN ROMANO CHEESE FRIES 60

WHO DOESN'T LOVE CHICKEN NUGGETS? EVER SINCE I WAS YOUNG THEY HAVE ALWAYS BEEN MY FAVORITE AFTERNOON SNACK AND NOW I HAVE MADE MY OWN VERSION WHICH WILL SAVE YOU BOTH TIME AND MONEY!

So Darn Good
Chicken Nuggets

THE STEPS

1. In a medium bowl add in the flour,
    salt and pepper, garlic powder and
    cheese. Set aside.

2. Heat the oil for about two minutes
    on medium-high heat.

3. Crack the eggs and place in a
    separate bowl.

4. Cut up the chicken into nugget size
    portions and toss in the flour mixture
    followed by the egg mixture and finally
    into the bread crumbs.

5. Cook until browned in small batches
    about a minute each.

6. Serve and enjoy.

SERVES 4-6

THE INGREDIENTS

4 boneless chicken breasts

1 cup of flour

Salt and pepper to taste

1 tsp of garlic powder

2 handfuls Parmesan cheese

2 eggs

1 cup of bread crumbs,
in a small bowl

1 cup of vegetable oil

A HEALTHIER VERSION THAN A TRADITIONAL QUESADILLA
AND IS BOUND TO BECOME A FAMILY FAVORITE!

TO ADD AN ITALIAN FLAIR, SERVE WITH BRUSCHETTA (see page 66)

Rosemary Balsamic Infused Quesadilla

THE STEPS

1. In a small bowl, mix the balsamic vinegar, rosemary, olive oil.

2. Melt butter in the pan.

3. Place the flour tortilla on pan and cook 1 minute per side.

4. Sprinkle the cheese on one ½ of the tortilla, place chicken onto cheese and fold tortilla in half.

5. Press firmly and flip until cheese is melted. Cut into four pieces and repeat until desired amount.

SERVES 1

THE INGREDIENTS

1 tbsp of butter

1 flour tortilla

¼ tsp balsamic vinegar

1 tbsp rosemary, chopped

½ cup of cooked chicken

Handful of Mozzarella cheese

Chicken Lo Mein

THE INGREDIENTS

2 (3 oz) packages of ramen noodle soup (toss out the flavor pack and cook according to directions, drain)

1 tbsp butter

1 tbsp garlic

1 boneless chicken breast

Salt and pepper to taste

1 cup of chicken broth

1 can mixed vegetables (corn, peas, green beans, carrots)

2 tbsp soy sauce

1 egg

THE STEPS

1. In a large skillet, heat the butter and cook the garlic until browned. Add in the chicken seasoning with salt and pepper (not too much) and cook for 3 minutes on each side. Now dice up the chicken and toss it back in the pan.

2. Add in the mixed veggies and stir in the chicken broth, noodles, and soy sauce.

3. The broth should absorb as it cooks, when it does push everything to the back of the pan and cook the egg. Break up the egg as it cooks and mix everything together and serve on medium size plates.

SERVES 4

THIS ONE IS SURE TO BE A HIT WITH THE KIDS. I AM POSITIVE YOU GUYS ORDER OUT AT LEAST ONCE A MONTH IF NOT ONCE A WEEK. WELL, THIS MEAL WILL SAVE YOU A FEW BUCKS! IT'S A UNDER $5 MEAL FOR TWO TO FOUR PEOPLE AND WILL MAKE YOU THINK TWICE ABOUT EATING OUT.

I FIRST CAME UP WITH THIS RECIPE WHEN I WASN'T SURE HOW TO FRY FRENCH FRIES. IN HIGH SCHOOL I WAS A BIG CHEESE FRY KINDA DUDE AND WOULD BUY A LARGE FRY FROM THE PLACE WITH THE ARCHES, GO HOME TOSS THEM ON A PLATE AND PUT SOME HERBS, A LITTLE GARLIC AND THROW SOME PECORINO ROMANO CHEESE ON TOP. HEAT IT UP IN THE MICRO FOR ABOUT A MINUTE AND LET IT RIP. ANYWAY...HERE IS THE TRUE VERSION!

Parmesan Romano Cheese Fries

THE STEPS

1. Slice the potatoes into french fries and place them in a large bowl of cold water. Set aside.

2. In a medium mixing bowl sift the flour.

3. Add in the spices and mix well.

4. Drop the potatoes into the flour mixture a little at a time and coat.

5. In a large skillet, heat the oil over medium-high heal.

6. Cook the fries until browned and crispy, flipping them as needed.

7. Place the fries that are done on a large plate layered with paper towels.

8. Preheat the oven to broil.

9. Transfer the fries onto a large baking sheet.

10. Top with the cheeses and broil until the cheese has melted.

11. Serve and definitely enjoy!

SERVES 4-6

THE INGREDIENTS

2 pounds of russet potatoes

1 cup of flour

1 tsp garlic powder

1 tsp salt

1 tsp pepper

1 tsp dried oregano

½ cup vegetable oil for frying

¼ cup shredded Romano cheese

½ cup shredded Parmesan cheese

CHAPTER FIVE

IT'S A DINNER PARTY

Good Evening,

A dinner party is one of my favorite things because you get to show your friends and family where you live and show off your wonderful culinary dishes. I have put together a nice selection of my favorite dishes in this chapter for you and your guests to enjoy. The theme for the night — simple yet elegant!

Let's get to it!

Pat

Tonight's Menu
Appetizers

TOMATO BRUSCHETTA 66
GENOA POTATO SKINS 68

Main Course & Sides

SALAMI WRAPPED CHICKEN
IN A RED WINE SAUCE 70
SERVED WITH ITALIAN
HEARTBURN POTATOES 74

PAN SEARED STEAK 72
WITH BRUSCHETTA
SERVED WITH SWEET
POTATO FRIES 76

Desserts

BANANAS FOSTER 78 OR
PUMPKIN PIE MOOSE 80

Tomato Bruschetta

3 tbsp of extra virgin olive oil

2 cloves of garlic, chopped

Salt and pepper to taste

4 basil leaves, diced

2 cans of petite diced tomatoes with olive oil, garlic & oregano, drained

2 tbsp of sweet Marsala wine

1 tbsp hot sauce

¼ cup shredded Parmesan cheese

1 French baguette

THE STEPS

1. In a large mixing bowl, combine all ingredients and place in the refrigerator for an hour.

2. Meanwhile, slice the baguette on a diagonal into ½ inch thick slices.

3. Coat one side of each slice with olive oil using a pastry brush. Place on a cooking sheet, olive oil side up and broil until browned for about one minute. Keep an eye on it, you don't want it to burn.

4. Place on a serving plate, top with the tomato mixture right before serving.

SERVES 6
PREP 10 MINUTES
TOTAL 1 HOUR & 10 MINUTES

AH... TOMATO BRUSCHETTA, AN ITALIAN FAVORITE. I LOVE THIS ONE BECAUSE I CAN MAKE THIS RECIPE AND GIVE IT TO FRIENDS AND FAMILY AS GIFTS. I LOVE THE AFTER BITE OF THE HOT SAUCE AND THE SWEETNESS FROM THE MARSALA WINE. THIS IS A VERY EASY RECIPE THAT YOU WILL LOVE TO SERVE AT FUTURE GATHERINGS AND PASS DOWN FROM GENERATION TO GENERATION.

Genoa Potato Skins

THE STEPS

1. Cut each potato in half, lengthwise. Using a spoon carefully take out about 60% of each potato so it looks like a boat.

2. In a small bowl, melt the butter in the microwave and brush each potato with the butter and season with salt and pepper. Set aside.

3. Roll each slice of salami into a roll and cut into five even sections (each section wraps around the potato boat).

4. Wrap the salami evenly on each skin (look at the picture to your left). Top each potato evenly with the cheese and season with thyme.

5. Arrange the potatoes on a baking sheet and place in the broiler for 5 minutes or until crispy.

6. ENJOY!

MAKES 8 SKINS
TOTAL 15 MINUTES

THE INGREDIENTS

4 yukon gold potatoes, cooked 4 minutes per side in the microwave

½ stick of butter

Salt and pepper to taste

2 slices of Genoa salami

8 oz of Pepper Jack cheese

1 sprig fresh thyme with stems removed

Salami Wrapped Chicken in a Red Wine Sauce

THE INGREDIENTS

2 tbsp margarine

4 thinly sliced chicken breasts

4 slices of Genoa salami, sliced thin

2 slices of Provolone cheese

4 tbsp olive oil

1 can of tomato paste

½ cup red wine

1 cup of crushed tomatoes

THE STEPS

1. In a large sauté pan, melt the butter and cook the chicken for four minutes per side.

2. Take out the chicken, leave the flame on and place ½ slice of provolone on top of each piece of chicken.

3. Wrap each chicken with salami and put back in the pan for 30 seconds per side, reduce heat to low.

4. Meanwhile, in a blender, add the olive oil, tomato paste and red wine. Blend until smooth and add to the pan.

5. Stir in the crushed tomatoes and heat for 3 minutes on medium high and serve.

SERVES 4
PREP 4 MINUTES
ACTIVE 10 MINUTES
TOTAL 14 MINUTES

I ABSOLUTELY LOVE TO MAKE THIS DISH IN THE KITCHEN! SADLY, MY WIFE HATES SALAMI...GO FIGURE! ANYWAY, HOPE YOU LOVE IT, IF NOT, YOU MIGHT WANT TO TURN THE PAGE.

Pan Seared Steak with Bruschetta

4 round steaks

½ cup butter or margarine

¼ cup flour to coat

Salt and pepper to taste

1 tsp garlic powder

1 cup of leftover
Tomato Bruschetta
(see page 66)

THE STEPS

1. Pound steak to make tender.

2. Put flour on cutting board, sprinkle salt and pepper evenly but lightly on both sides of each steak. Coat steak with the flour.

3. Melt butter in a large skillet and cook for 5 minutes per side.

4. Top each steak with ¼ cup bruschetta.

5. Serve and eat.

SERVES 4
PREP 2 MINUTES
ACTIVE 10 MINUTES
TOTAL 12 MINUTES

WHO NEEDS A GRILL WHEN YOU HAVE A SAUTÉ PAN OR FRYING PAN? JUST MELT SOME BUTTER, SEASON A CUT OF MEAT WITH SALT AND PEPPER AND COAT IN SOME FLOUR. WE'RE JUST GOING TO TOP IT WITH SOME LEFTOVER BRUSCHETTA :) (see page 66)

Italian Heartburn Potatoes

THE INGREDIENTS

1 bag of frozen, cubed hash brown potatoes

1 can cream of chicken soup

1 stick of butter, melted

1 tbsp of minced garlic

2 large basil leaves, chopped

1 cup of freshly shredded Mozzarella cheese

1 cup of freshly shredded Cheddar cheese

1 tbsp fresh rosemary, chopped

1 tbsp fresh parsley, chopped

16 oz sour cream

THE STEPS

1. Preheat the oven to 300°F.

2. In a large bowl, combine all ingredients and mix well.

3. Place in a casserole dish and place in the oven.

4. Set the timer for 70 min.

5. Take it out of the oven and let sit for 5 minutes before serving.

SERVES 8-10
PREP 10 MINUTES
ACTIVE 70 MINUTES
TOTAL 80 MINUTES

THIS RECIPE IS A SPIN-OFF FROM A DISH IN MY FIRST BOOK. THIS TIME I PUT AN ITALIAN FLAIR ON THIS HENCE THE NAME. ANYWAY, THIS ONE KNOCKS IT RIGHT OUT OF THE PARK FOR ALL OF MY GUESTS. AS HOPEFULLY, IT WILL IT FOR YOURS.

THESE ARE BOUND TO BE THAT NEW SIDE DISH YOUR FAMILY WILL ASK YOU FOR! BEST PART IS — IT'S HEALTHY TOO! SO GATHER 'ROUND FOR SOME YUMMY FRIES.

Sweet Potato Fries with a hint of Cinnamon

THE STEPS

1. Preheat the oven to 375°F.

2. Place the cut sweet potatoes into a microwave-safe dish filled with water.

3. Cook on high in the microwave for 5 minutes.

4. Drain off liquid using a colander, toss with cinnamon, sea salt and olive oil. Arrange fries on a baking sheet in a single layer.

5. Bake for 30 minutes, turning half-way through.

SERVES 4
PREP 10 MINUTES
ACTIVE 30 MINUTES
TOTAL 40 MINUTES

THE INGREDIENTS

4 sweet potatoes, cut into large french fries

1 tbsp water

½ tbsp cinnamon powder

1 pinch of sea salt

2 tbsp olive oil

77

THIS IS ALWAYS A HAPPY ENDING FOR ANY MEAL
AND IT MAKES THE KITCHEN SMELL WONDERFUL!

Bananas Foster

THE STEPS

1. In a large frying pan, melt the butter and stir in the brown sugar, cinnamon, and vanilla extract.

2. Stir until the sugar dissolves and add in the bananas. Cook for one minute per side.

3. Remove the bananas from the pan and place into the serving dishes.

4. Slowly add in the rum, fair warning, IT WILL FLAME.

5. Cook until the flame runs out, about 1 minute.

6. Turn off the flame, stir and remove the pan from the heat.

7. Place two scoops of ice cream onto each serving dish. Using a spoon, top with the sauce.

8. Enjoy!

SERVES 2
PREP 2 MINUTES
TOTAL 10 MINUTES

THE INGREDIENTS

½ stick of butter

1 cup of brown sugar

1 tsp cinnamon powder

¼ cup dark rum

1 tsp vanilla extract

2 large bananas cut lengthwise, then in half

4 scoops of vanilla ice cream

FOR ALL OF THOSE YEAR-ROUND THANKSGIVING LOVERS THIS ONE IS FOR YOU! IT'S A MODERN TWIST ON A CLASSIC TREAT IN MOUSSE FORM, WHICH MAKES IT EVEN BETTER. FOR A SOPHISTICATED EVENING, SERVE IN A MARTINI GLASS AND TOP WITH A GRAHAM CRACKER.

Pumpkin Pie Mousse

THE STEPS

1. In a large, cold mixing bowl using a cold whisk make whipped cream using the sugar and heavy cream for about 5 minutes (or if you're like me, one song on the radio should do it).

2. Add in the pumpkin pie filling, cinnamon powder, and vanilla extract.

3. In a small resealable bag, smash the crackers.

4. I serve this in large martini glasses and usually get about 4 servings. To start the distribution, add the crushed graham crackers evenly into the glasses.

5. Next, distribute the filing evenly into each glass.

6. To serve it, sprinkle with cinnamon.

SERVES 4

THE INGREDIENTS

½ cup of sugar

1 pint of whipping cream

1 (29 oz) can of pumpkin pie filling (pumpkin puree)

2 tsp cinnamon powder

1 tsp vanilla extract

8 graham crackers (2 sheets)

CHAPTER SIX

NEW ITA STY

Buon Giorno!

Come sta? *(Hello everyone how are you?)* Ah the beauty of the Italian language. But you know what's better then the Italian language? The Italian food.

So in this chapter we will be cooking some of the food from my heritage...Well 25% of my heritage. It's easy, it's fun and it's comforting — it is my favorite section in this book! We have everything from classic dishes like **Married for the Meatballs** and the **Old-fashioned Tomato Pie** to modern twists on **Italian Tacos** and the **Roman-style Buffalo Chicken Dip**.

I dedicate this chapter to my family because the best memories are always made at the kitchen table in my family. When I was younger we used to go to my grandma Dinucci's every Sunday morning where she would cook us anything we wanted. She passed away back in 2005 and now we go to my to my Mom- Moms where we do the same thing. The tradition continues with the next generation as one day it will go to my generation.

Anyway, it is with great pleasure that I give you the New Italian Style section. Just remember, it's an *Italian thing* so kick back and grab a glass of wine. :)

Let's get cooking, Bella!

Pat

Chef's Specials

MARRIED FOR THE MEATBALLS 86

OLD-FASHIONED TOMATO PIE 88

SUMMERTIME CHICKEN 90

LOW-FAT CHICKEN ALFREDO 92

PENNE PASTA IN AN ORANGE CREAM SAUCE 94

RAVIOLI IN A SPINACH CREAM SAUCE 96

THREE-CHEESE RISOTTO 98

ITALIAN TACOS 100

ROMAN-STYLE BUFFALO CHICKEN DIP 102

THIS IS MY FAVORITE RECIPE! THERE IS NOTHING LIKE A FAMILY CLASSIC BUT I LIKE TO MAKE IT A LITTLE DIFFERENT. I THINK EVERYONE IN MY FAMILY MAKES MEATBALLS IN A DIFFERENT WAY, WHICH MAKES US ALL UNIQUE. I AM THE ONLY ONE WHO MAKES THEM WITH FRESH HERBS INSTEAD OF THE USUAL DRIED MIX. THE KEY INGREDIENT THOUGH IS THE ROSEMARY. TRUST ME ON THIS ONE ;) THE STORY BEHIND THE NAME COMES FROM MY WIFE — SHE ALWAYS USES MY ITALIAN MEATBALLS AS THE KEY THAT WON HER OVER.

Married for the Meatballs

THE STEPS

1. In a large mixing bowl, add in all of the ingredients and mix well using your hands so that all of the flavors blend together.

2. Shape into meatballs. The recipe should make about 25.

3. In a large skillet, fry in olive oil in batches of 8.

4. Fry until browned, about 8 minutes a batch.

BASIC TOMATO SAUCE

1. Combine all ingredients in a medium sauce pan.

2. Heat for 6-8 minutes on medium-high heat, stirring occasionally.

SERVES 6-8
PREP 15 MINUTES
COOK 6-8 MINUTES PER BATCH
TOTAL 40 MINUTES

THE INGREDIENTS

MEATBALLS

2 lbs of meatloaf mix (ground pork, beef, and veal)

2 tbsp of minced garlic

2 splashes of milk

1 egg

2-3 handfuls of grated Romano Cheese

2 handfuls of parsley, chopped

1 tbsp rosemary, chopped

1 cup of olive oil

1 cup Italian bread crumbs

SAUCE

1 can of crushed tomatoes

1 can of roasted garlic tomato paste

¼ cup olive oil

6 basil leaves

1 garlic clove, chopped

ALL RIGHT, IT MIGHT GET A LITTLE MESSY IN HERE!
THIS RECIPE IS GREAT FOR FRIDAY NIGHT DINNERS.
IT IS TRADITION IN MY HOUSEHOLD TO SERVE IT
AT LEAST ONCE A MONTH. IT'S PRETTY SIMPLE AND
YOU'LL SAVE SOME CASH FOR DESSERT. ;)

Old-Fashioned Tomato Pie

New Italian Style

1. Preheat the oven to 450°F.

2. On a large cutting board, press out the dough so it looks like a frisbee. Using your fists, stretch the dough into a pizza shape.

3. Slide the dough onto a pizza stone and brush with olive oil and thyme.

4. In a medium mixing bowl, add all the sauce ingredients and stir.

5. Using a ladle top the sauce onto the pizza and add the cheese.

6. Bake for 15-20 minutes let cool and serve.

SERVES 4
PREP 10 MINUTES
COOK 15-20 MINUTES
TOTAL 25-30 MINUTES

THE INGREDIENTS

CRUST

1 thawed ball of pizza dough raised according to package

Flour for dusting

2 tbsp olive oil

Handful of thyme

SAUCE

1 can of crushed tomatoes

1 tbsp of minced garlic

Handful of fresh basil, finely chopped

TOPPING

5 slices of Mozzarella cheese

Summertime Chicken

THE INGREDIENTS

4 tbsp olive oil

2 tbsp fresh rosemary, sliced and diced

1 tbsp fresh thyme

3 tbsp of garlic

4 chicken breasts thinly sliced

Salt and pepper to taste

½ cup of white wine

THE STEPS

1. In a medium pan, add the olive oil, rosemary, thyme and the garlic. Heat until garlic is browned.

2. Add in the chicken seasoning with salt and pepper and cook two minutes per side.

3. Add in the white wine and let simmer.

4. Arrange the chicken on a long serving plate and pour the sauce over the top.

5. Serve it up and enjoy!

SERVES 4
PREP 7 MINUTES
ACTIVE 13 MINUTES
TOTAL 20 MINUTES

THIS IS A REALLY SIMPLE AND FAST RECIPE FOR WHEN YOU ARE HAVING SOME COMPANY OVER. SINCE IT GETS DONE PRETTY FAST, THERE IS MORE TIME TO SPEND CHATTING ABOUT THE LATEST GOSSIP IN TOWN. WHAT'S GREAT IS THAT IT USES ALL FRESH HERBS SO YOU CAN JUST IMAGINE HOW GREAT IT MUST SMELL! SO WHAT ARE YOU WAITING FOR? LET'S MAKE SOME SUMMERTIME CHICKEN!

*ITALIAN HEARTBURN POTATOES (see page 74)
COMPLIMENT THIS DISH VERY WELL!

Low-Fat Chicken Alfredo

THE INGREDIENTS

4 tbsp butter

1 tbsp minced garlic

Salt and pepper to taste

4 thinly sliced
chicken breasts

¼ cup parsley, finely chopped

¼ cup dry white wine

1 block of Neufchatel
cream cheese

¾ cup Parmesan cheese

1 lb fettuccine pasta, cooked

THE STEPS

1. In a medium skillet over medium heat melt the butter and add in the garlic, salt and pepper. Heat until the garlic is browned. Cook the chicken for 2 minutes per side.

2. Add in the parsley and white wine and put heat on medium-high to let the wine cook off for about 3 minutes.

3. Add in the Neufchatel cheese stirring constantly until melted, for about a minute.

4. Stir in the Parmesan cheese and add in the cooked pasta.

5. Serve and eat.

SERVES 6-8
PREP 10 MINUTES
ACTIVE 15 MINUTES
TOTAL 25 MINUTES

THIS IS ONE OF MY WIFE'S FAVORITE DISHES BUT I ONLY MAKE IT ON SPECIAL OCCASIONS BECAUSE IT IS NOT THE HEALTHIEST OF RECIPES. BECAUSE OF THAT, I HAVE CUT OUT A LOT OF THE FAT AS I HAVE FOUND THE ART OF SUBSTITUTING THE HEAVY CREAM WITH THE NEUFCHATEL CHEESE (LOW-FAT CREAM CHEESE).

THIS RECIPE IS TO DIE FOR! ONE OF MY ALL TIME FAVORITES!
THE SECRET IN THIS RECIPE IS THE SALTINESS OF THE PANCETTA AND
THE ORANGE JUICE WHICH ADDS A LITTLE BIT OF A TANGY SWEETNESS.
SWEET AND SALTY! HMM — SOUNDS LIKE A PRETTY GOOD COMBO!
THE PARSLEY AND GARLIC MAKE IT PRETTY GOOD AS WELL :)

Penne Pasta with Pancetta in an Orange and Wine Cream Sauce

New Italian Style

THE STEPS

1. In a medium skillet over medium heat, melt the butter and add in the garlic, salt and pepper, heat until garlic and pancetta is browned.

2. Add in the parsley, white wine and orange juice and put heat on medium-high to let the wine cook off for about 3 minutes.

3. Stir in the cheese and pasta.

4. Serve and eat.

SERVES 6-8
PREP 10 MINUTES
COOK 15 MINUTES
TOTAL 25 MINUTES

THE INGREDIENTS

4 tbsp butter

1 tbsp minced garlic

Salt and pepper to taste

2 slices of pancetta or bacon, sliced and diced

¼ cup basil, chopped and diced

½ cup dry white wine

¼ cup orange juice

1 lb of penne pasta, cooked

95

Ravioli in a Spinach Cream Sauce

THE INGREDIENTS

2 tbsp butter

¼ cup chicken broth

¼ cup of Romano cheese

2 garlic cloves

¼ tsp sea salt

1 cup of low-fat
Cream cheese

Salt and pepper to taste

2 cups of cooked spinach

1 (13 oz) package of
cooked ravioli

THE STEPS

1. In a food processor, add the butter, chicken broth, Romano cheese, garlic, sea salt and cream cheese and blend until smooth.

2. In a large sauté pan, simmer the heavy cream until slightly thickened.

3. Add in the spinach and cooked ravioli.

SERVES 4
TOTAL 20 MINUTES

THIS IS AN ENTRÉE VERSION OF THE ROASTED GARLIC SPINACH DIP RECIPE WHICH YOU WILL SEE LATER ON IN THE BOOK.

RISOTTO IS JUST ABOUT ONE OF THE COOLEST THINGS TO MAKE. THE BEST THING ABOUT IT, IS THERE ARE ENDLESS POSSIBILITIES OF THINGS TO CREATE! THIS IS JUST ONE OF THE BASICS THAT YOU WILL FIND IN A FINE DINING ITALIAN RESTAURANT. THE CHEESE MAKES THE DISH TASTE SO GOOD! THE FRESH ITALIAN HERBS — MAMMA MIA! I CAN SMELL IT NOW. THE BEST PART: **NO RESERVATION REQUIRED!**

Three-Cheese Risotto

THE STEPS

1. In a large sauté pan, melt the butter and olive oil on medium heat.

2. Once the butter is melted, add in the onion and garlic. Cook until browned.

3. Add in the rice and wine, stirring occasionally for two minutes.
    Then add in 1 cup of the broth and stir constantly for 2 minutes.

4. Once the broth has absorbed the previous ingredients, add in the rest of the broth and the herbs and cook for 15 minutes.

5. Finally, add in the cheeses and cook for an additional 3 minutes, stirring occasionally.

6. Plate it up on four dishes and enjoy.

SERVES 4-6
PREP 5 MINUTES
COOK 20 MINUTES
TOTAL 25 MINUTES

THE INGREDIENTS

2 tbsp extra virgin olive oil

½ stick of margarine

1 medium onion, sliced and diced

2 cups Arborio rice

½ cup white wine

3 cups of chicken broth

1 tsp each of thyme, basil, and rosemary

¼ cup each grated Parmesan, Romano, and Mozzarella cheeses

Italian Tacos

THE INGREDIENTS

8 taco shells

1 lb of **meatballs**
(see page 87)

1 cup of your favorite
tomato sauce

1 ½ cups of Parmesan
cheese

1 cup of arugula

1 cup of **Tomato
Bruschetta**
(see page 66)

THE STEPS

1. Heat the meatballs in a medium skillet
    over medium-high heat for 8 minutes,
    flipping as needed.

2. Break up the meatballs (you want
    them smashed before you do the
    next step).

3. Add in the tomato sauce and stir
    constantly for 3 minutes, then turn
    off the heat.

4. Heat the taco shells according to
    the package and top with meat
    followed by the cheese, arugula
    and Bruschetta.

SERVES 4
PREP 7 MINUTES
ACTIVE 13 MINUTES
TOTAL 20 MINUTES

HAVE YOU EVER WONDERED HOW TO MODERNIZE THE AVERAGE TACO INTO A NEW ITALIAN CLASSIC? WELL YOUR PRAYERS HAVE BEEN ANSWERED! FOR THIS ONE, TRY USING YOUR CLASSIC ITALIAN INGREDIENTS: MEATBALLS, PARMESAN, BRUSCHETTA, ARUGULA! LADIES AND GENTS, I GIVE YOU ITALIAN TACOS. I GUARANTEE THIS IS SOON TO BE A FAMILY FAVORITE AT YOUR DINNER TABLE SO GO AHEAD AND GIVE IT A TRY.

Roman-style Buffalo Chicken Dip

THE STEPS

1. Preheat the oven to 375°F.

2. In a medium mixing bowl, combine the chicken, ranch, hot sauce and Cheddar cheese.

3. In a small bowl, remove the Neufchatel cheese from the foil wrapper and place in the microwave. Heat for 30 seconds or until softened.

4. Add the Neufchatel, rosemary, garlic and chicken broth to the chicken and ranch mixture.

5. Transfer into a casserole dish and place into the oven for 10-12 minutes.

6. Serve it up with crackers or chips.

SERVES 6-8
TOTAL 20 MINUTES

THE INGREDIENTS

1 (12.5 oz) canned white chicken breast

½ cup ranch dressing

½ cup hot sauce

½ cup sharp shredded Cheddar cheese

8 oz Neufchatel cheese

2 tbsp rosemary, diced

1 clove of garlic, diced

2 tbsp chicken broth

AN ITALIAN SPIN OFF ON A TRADITIONAL AMERICAN DIP, THE ROSEMARY AND GARLIC ADD AN AWESOME PUNCH WHICH IS BOUND TO MAKE THIS DISH A NEW ITALIAN CLASSIC.

CHAPTER SEVEN

MAN CAVE

Hey Fellas,

This one is for the sports fans! This chapter is filled with all of your favorite game day grub, plus some new favorites for you to enjoy!

My family and I are big tailgaters! We've been going to all the Penn State football games ever since I was a toddler and boy have I have learned a lot from watching them over the years! That's why I decided to put this chapter in here, it's my own spin on tailgating at home. When you pre-game at home, there are so many more possibilities with what you can make and in this section you will find everything from **Captain Jack's Nachos** to **Cheeseburger Risotto**. Yeah — I went there! It took a lot of hard work trying to figure out how to get it perfect but It was so worth it in the end.

If you are hosting a super bowl party or just going to a friend's house to watch the game, there is plenty of different types of food for everyone's taste buds.

So turn on that game, grab an ice cold beer and let's eat some great food for you are now entering The Man Cave!

Grub on!

Pat

Game Day Grub

JAMAICAN JERK CHICKEN CAKES 108

TOMATO & HERB DIP 110

CAPTAIN JACK'S NACHOS 112

TUSCANY MEETS NACHOS 114

CLASSIC CHILI NACHOS 116

TERIYAKI STEAK QUESADILLAS 118

CHEESEBURGER RISOTTO 120

ROASTED GARLIC SPINACH DIP 122

Jamaican Jerk Chicken Cakes

THE STEPS

1. In a large bowl, combine all of the ingredients EXCEPT THE BUTTER and mix with your hands as if you were making meatballs, then flatten them.

2. In a medium skillet, heat the butter over medium-high heat and place in the chicken patties.

3. Cook for 1 minute per side.

4. Serve and enjoy.

MAKES 4 CHICKEN CAKES

THE INGREDIENTS

1 cup Italian bread crumbs

2 cans of cooked chicken breast

1 tbsp Jamaican jerk sauce

4 tbsp mayo

1 egg

1 tbsp minced garlic

1 handful of fresh parsley

2 tbsp butter for frying

THIS ONE IS A PERSONAL FAVORITE AS WELL AS JUST PLAIN EASY TO MAKE. IT REMINDS ME OF A CRAB CAKE EXCEPT IT IS MORE AFFORDABLE. BEST PART IS THE CHICKEN IS ALREADY COOKED SO ALL YOU HAVE TO DO IS JUST BROWN THE CHICKEN CAKES.

Tomato & Herb Dip

THE INGREDIENTS

1 (6 oz) can of roasted garlic tomato paste

1 block of Neufchatel cheese

1 packet of onion dip mix

1 tbsp rosemary, chopped

2 tbsp minced garlic

1 splash of Pinot Noir Red Wine

1 (8 oz) container of sour cream

¼ cup Parmesan cheese

THE STEPS

1. Place all ingredients in a large blender and pulse until smooth for about 30 seconds.

2. Refrigerate for at least an hour before serving to guests.

3. Serve in a large bowl with pretzels or a sliced baguette.

SERVES 8-10

WHAT'S BETTER THAN MUNCHING ON CHIPS OR PRETZELS DURING A GAME? MUNCHING ON PRETZELS WITH THIS TOMATO & HERB DIP!

A TASTY LAST MINUTE RECIPE TO THROW TOGETHER WHEN YOU ARE HOSTING A FOOTBALL BASH.

Captain Jack's Nachos

THE STEPS

1. Place the chips on a serving plate.

2. Top evenly with the shredded cheese, garlic, Italian seasonings.

3. Drizzle the sauce over top of the nachos.

4. Cook for 1 minute in the microwave.

SERVES 4

THE INGREDIENTS

4 cups of Nacho cheese flavored tortilla chips

¾ cup freshly shredded Cheddar cheese

1 tsp minced garlic

1 tsp of fresh rosemary, diced

2 tbsp barbecue sauce

Tuscany Meets Nachos

THE INGREDIENTS

4 cups of cool ranch tortilla chips

½ cup of shredded Mozzarella cheese

¼ cup grated Parmesan cheese

1 tsp fresh rosemary

1 tsp garlic

2 tbsp ranch dressing

THE STEPS

1. On a serving plate place the chips.

2. Layer with the cheeses. Sprinkle with the rosemary and garlic. Drizzle ranch dressing on top.

3. Heat in the microwave for 1 minute.

4. Serve immediately.

SERVES 4

ITALY HAS INVADED MEXICO AND CREATED IT'S OWN ITALIAN STYLE
OF NACHOS AND IT'S BOUND TO GET THE CROWD WANTING SOME MORE!

MY OWN VERSION OF A CLASSIC DISH SERVED AT ALMOST EVERY PUB IN THE NATION IS NOW AT YOUR FINGERTIPS. TO ADD A TACO FLAIR TO THE NACHOS, ARRANGE THEM ATOP A BED OF CHOPPED LETTUCE.

Classic Chili Nachos

THE STEPS

1. Cook the beef with the taco seasoning.

2. On a serving plate, place the chips.

3. Layer with the cooked beef, salsa, peppers and cheese.

4. Heat in the microwave for 1 minute.

5. Serve immediately.

SERVES 4

THE INGREDIENTS

2 cups tortilla chips

¼ cup beef, cooked

1 tbsp taco seasoning

4 tbsp salsa (mild)

6 banana pepper rings, chopped

2 handfuls of shredded Mozzarella cheese

Salt and pepper to taste

Teriyaki Steak Quesadillas

THE INGREDIENTS

1 tbsp butter

1 flour tortilla

2 tbsp teriyaki sauce

½ cup cooked steak, chopped

Handful of Taco cheese

THE STEPS

1. Melt butter onto the pan.

2. Place the flour tortilla on pan and cook 1 minute per side.

3. Place a handful of Taco cheese on half of the tortilla.

4. Place meat on top of the cheese and fold tortilla in half.

5. Press firmly and flip until cheese is melted.

6. Cut into four pieces and repeat until desired amount.

SERVES 1

THIS DISH IS A WEEKLY TRADITION IN OUR HOUSE. IT'S ONE OF THE QUICKEST DISHES TO MAKE — SO EASY AND SO DELICIOUS! ENJOY!

Cheeseburger Risotto

THE STEPS

1. In a large skillet, heat the oil and butter over medium heat and add in the onion. Cook until browned.

2. Add in the rice and about ½ cup of the broth. Stir and let the rice absorb the broth.

3. Add in the remaining broth, ½ cup at a time, stirring constantly.

4. Add in the parsley, cheese, beef, bacon, tomato paste, and barbecue sauce.

5. Let simmer stirring every 3 minutes.

6. Cook for 18 minutes total.

7. Serve immediately on small plates.

SERVES 4

THE INGREDIENTS

2 tbsp olive oil

2 tbsp of butter

1 medium onion, peeled and diced

2 cups risotto rice

2 cups of beef broth

2 handfuls of fresh parsley

½ cup of shredded Cheddar cheese

½ lb ground beef, cooked and chopped

3 slices of bacon, cooked and diced

4 tbsp of tomato paste with roasted garlic

3 tbsp your favorite barbecue sauce

Roasted Garlic Spinach Dip

THE INGREDIENTS

15 oz whole milk Ricotta cheese

12 oz French onion dip

2 tbsp ranch dressing

1 tsp lemon juice

1 tsp hot sauce

¼ cup Parmesan cheese

1 tsp garlic powder

Salt and pepper to taste

1 (9 oz) package of frozen spinach (cooked according to package)

THE STEPS

1. In a large bowl combine the Ricotta cheese, onion dip, ranch dressing, and the lemon juice, mix well using a wooden spoon.

2. Add in the Parmesan cheese, garlic, salt and pepper, and the cooked spinach.

3. Mix well.

4. Refrigerate for about 1 hour before serving.

SERVES 6-8

CHAPTER EIGHT

Dear Friends,

At the beginning of this journey, I promised you a Coffee Shop chapter, well here it is! This section is among my favorites because I am a big coffee fan, I drink a lot of it each day, though that's probably not a good thing, but oh well, it's my thing!

Most of this chapter consists of coffee drinks, served hot or iced that you can make at home and I promise you, they will taste even better than those you get at coffee-houses near you. Best part is you won't have to pay big bucks to get a taste of these delicious and refreshing drinks!

At the end, you'll find a special treat, one of my prized desserts that is super easy to make and a great dessert to finish off any meal in this book.

Salute! _Pat_

CoffeeShop

MORNING TIME
RUSH ICED MOCHA 128

SALTED CARAMEL
HOT CHOCOLATE 130

MOCHA FRAPPÉ 132

CARAMEL ZEPPOLES
WITH A HAZELNUT
CRÉME SAUCE 134

Morning Time Rush Iced Mocha

THE STEPS

1. In a 10 oz glass, add the hot chocolate mix, coffee, milk and stir until blended.

2. Toss in the ice cubes and stir in some sugar.

3. Drink and enjoy.

SERVES 1

THE INGREDIENTS

2 tbsp chocolate syrup

1 cup of fresh brewed coffee

$\frac{1}{3}$ cup cold milk

6 ice cubes

Sugar to taste

SKIP OUT ON THE MORNING RUSH AT THE LOCAL COFFEE SHOP AND MAKE THIS SUMMERTIME FAVORITE AT HOME WITH NO LINE AND BEST OF ALL YOU DON'T HAVE TO WASTE ANY GAS!

THIS DRINK IS JUST PLAIN AND SIMPLE, YET VERY BOLD IN FLAVOR AND IT WILL SAVE EVERYONE MONEY. I LOVE THE WAY THE CARAMEL COMPLIMENTS THE CHOCOLATE AND THE SALT ON TOP IS JUST PURE EVIL.

Salted Caramel Hot Chocolate

Coffee Shop

THE STEPS

1. In a large coffee cup add the caramel syrup and hot chocolate mix. Stir in the steamed milk.

2. Top with your favorite whipped cream.

3. Drizzle with caramel sauce or chocolate syrup.

4. Top with dash of salt and serve.

SERVES 1

THE INGREDIENTS

1 tbsp caramel flavored syrup

1 packet of hot chocolate mix

1 cup of steamed milk

Whipped cream for topping

Drizzle of caramel sauce or chocolate syrup

Dash of fine salt

Mocha Frappé

THE INGREDIENTS

½ cup semi-sweet chocolate chips

1 pkg hot chocolate mix

$\frac{1}{3}$ cup Half and Half

1 cup ice

¼ cup fresh coffee

Whipped cream

Chocolate syrup

THE STEPS

1. In a blender, mix all ingredients and blend on frappé mode.

2. Between two glasses, add the drink mixture.

3. Top with whipped cream and chocolate syrup.

SERVES 1

NOW THE LATEST COFFEE TREND CAN BE MADE AT HOME AND ALL YOU NEED IS A BLENDER (YEAH IT'S THAT EASY) AND DON'T FORGET TO SERVE IT IN A REUSABLE CUP.

FOR A CARAMEL VERSION, SUBSTITUTE WITH CARAMEL CHIPS AND CARAMEL SYRUP.

Caramel Zeppoles with a Hazelnut Créme Sauce

THE INGREDIENTS

ZEPPOLES

1 package of premade pizza dough ball, thawed

½ cup sugar

2 tbsp caramel syrup

4 tbsp olive oil for frying

DIPPING SAUCE

½ cup sugar

½ cup water

1 cup hazelnut creamer

Dash of salt

THE STEPS

1. After the dough rises on a large cutting board, roll out the dough to make the zeppoles.

2. Oil your hands with olive oil; cut each piece of dough into a 1 inch ball; stretch and twist it and let it sit for 3 minutes.

3. Fry in batches of 8-10 in a frying pan with the olive oil until lightly browned.

4. After the zeppoles have cooled, in a large bowl toss with the sugar and caramel.

5. For the sauce, simmer the sugar and water for 8 minutes swirling every 2 minutes. Turn off the heat and stir in the hazelnut creamer and salt.

MAKES 10-16

FIRST AND FOREMOST WHAT EXACTLY IS A ZEPPOLI?
WELL IT IS PRETTY SIMPLE! IT'S A DELICIOUS BITE SIZE
FRIED PIZZA DESSERT. THERE ARE ENDLESS POSSIBILITIES
AS TO WHAT TO MIX WITH IT. I STICK TO BASICS; SUGAR BUT
WITH A TWIST — I MIX IN CARAMEL SYRUP AND MAKE A
HAZELNUT DIPPING SAUCE THIS IS PERFECT WITH A CUP
OF ESPRESSO.

HOME
COOKING

that will please you

Special thanks to:

The love of my life and soon to be wife, Julie for having to put up with me first thing in the morning! Julie I Love You!

My mother and father for bringing me into this world and for always believing in me.

My grandmother for always letting me help her in the kitchen.

Edyta, for putting the pieces together for a second time I might add and for taking these beautiful photos!

Mrs. Liv and Mrs. Morgan, my culinary teachers from high school, for inspiring me and helping me fall even more in love with food!

Mr. Richard Kozlowski for supporting me and letting me put this new book in his store.

EXTRA SPECIAL THANKS TO MY TASTE-TESTERS: Julie, Danielle, Dennis, Sean, Dana, The Liz, Mom, Dad, Rich, Eric, Jen and Edyta

Also my **publishing company** as well as **amazon.com**.

I would like to thank **anyone and everyone** who helped me out on this journey, to all the teachers I had in high school who knew I would do something big in my life. It makes me so happy to know you believed in me! Thank you!

Oh! And last, but certainly not least…**YOU**! Thank YOU for purchasing a copy of this cookbook. Thank you for taking a chance on me and I hope you stick around for the rest of the ride as there's sure to be plenty more to come in the future. I hope this book brings you and your family closer as you make new and exciting memories in the kitchen and find new favorite recipes to pass down to your friends, neighbors, and of course, your loved ones!

Here's to you!

Until next time,

Patrick Fisher

Patrick Fisher
No Reservation Required

© 2012, Patrick Fisher

Content by Patrick Fisher
Original photography by Edyta Kuciapa
Designed and typeset by Edyta Kuciapa

NO RESERVATION REQUIRED

Made in the USA
Las Vegas, NV
14 May 2024